ALL ABOUT ARACHNIDS
WOLF SPIDERS

by Becca Becker

pogo

Ideas for Parents and Teachers

Pogo Books let children practice reading informational text while introducing them to nonfiction features such as headings, labels, sidebars, maps, and diagrams, as well as a table of contents, glossary, and index.

Carefully leveled text with a strong photo match offers early fluent readers the support they need to succeed.

Before Reading

- "Walk" through the book and point out the various nonfiction features. Ask the student what purpose each feature serves.
- Look at the glossary together. Read and discuss the words.

Read the Book

- Have the child read the book independently.
- Invite them to list questions that arise from reading.

After Reading

- Discuss the child's questions. Talk about how they might find answers to those questions.
- Prompt the child to think more. Ask: What did you know about wolf spiders before reading this book? What more would you like to learn about them?

Pogo Books are published by Jump!
5357 Penn Avenue South
Minneapolis, MN 55419
www.jumplibrary.com

Copyright © 2025 Jump!
International copyright reserved in all countries. No part of this book may be reproduced in any form without written permission from the publisher.

Library of Congress Cataloging-in-Publication Data

Names: Becker, Becca, author.
Title: Wolf spiders / by Becca Becker.
Description: Minneapolis, MN: Jump!, Inc., [2025]
Series: All about arachnids | Includes index.
Audience: Ages 7-10
Identifiers: LCCN 2024032968 (print)
LCCN 2024032969 (ebook)
ISBN 9798892136303 (hardcover)
ISBN 9798892136310 (paperback)
ISBN 9798892136327 (ebook)
Subjects: LCSH: Wolf spiders—Juvenile literature.
Classification: LCC QL458.42.L9 B43 2025 (print)
LCC QL458.42.L9 (ebook)
DDC 595.4/4—dc23/eng/20240830
LC record available at https://lccn.loc.gov/2024032968
LC ebook record available at https://lccn.loc.gov/2024032969

Editor: Katie Chanez
Designer: Emma Almgren-Bersie

Photo Credits: Chase D'animulls/iStock, cover; Tobias Hauke/Shutterstock, 1; Piotr Velixar/Shutterstock, 3; spxChrome/iStock, 4; Elliotte Rusty Harold/Shutterstock, 5; Bryan Reynolds/Alamy, 6-7; Macrolife/iStock, 8-9; Macronatura/Shutterstock, 10-11; Henrik Larsson/Shutterstock, 12; Lightwriter1949/iStock, 13; Andrew Ring/Shutterstock, 14-15; Chase D'animulls/Shutterstock, 16; Vinicius Souza/Alamy, 17; blickwinkel/Alamy, 18-19; CathyKeifer/iStock, 20-21; arlindo71/iStock, 23.

Printed in the United States of America at Corporate Graphics in North Mankato, Minnesota.

TABLE OF CONTENTS

CHAPTER 1
Sprinting Spiders 4

CHAPTER 2
Spiderlings 12

CHAPTER 3
Chasing Prey 16

ACTIVITIES & TOOLS
Try This! 22
Glossary 23
Index 24
To Learn More 24

CHAPTER 1
SPRINTING SPIDERS

A spider **sprints** across the ground. Its eight thin legs are fast. This **arachnid** runs up to two feet (0.6 meters) in one second. What is it? It is a wolf spider!

There are more than 2,300 wolf spider **species**. Some are tan or brown. Others are black or gray. Many have stripes on their bodies. Their coloring helps them blend in.

CHAPTER 1

The Carolina wolf spider is one of the largest. Its **leg span** is almost three inches (7.6 centimeters).

DID YOU KNOW?

The Carolina wolf spider can bite. Its fangs have **venom**. The venom does not harm people. But it will make people itch!

CHAPTER 1 7

chelicerae

Wolf spiders are known for their long legs. They have strong jaws called chelicerae. These help the spider hold **prey**. At the tips of them are sharp fangs.

TAKE A LOOK!

What are the parts of a wolf spider? Take a look!

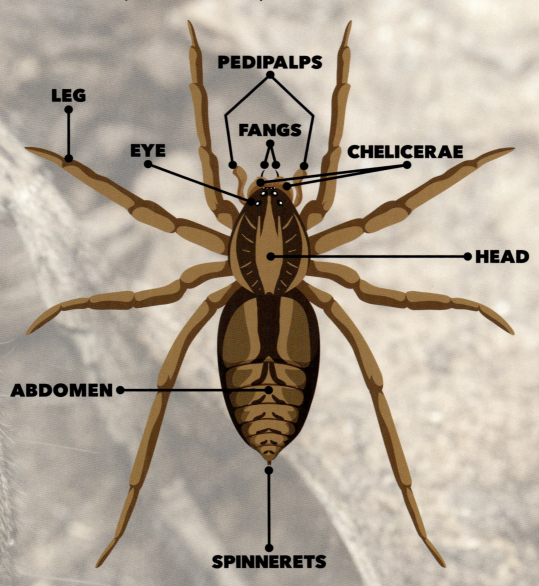

CHAPTER 1

Some wolf spiders dig **burrows**. They live in them. Others stay safe under logs and rocks.

DID YOU KNOW?

Wolf spiders can live almost anywhere. Some live on cold mountains. Others live in **grasslands**. They also live in hot deserts and wet rain forests. They live on lawns and in fields, too.

CHAPTER 2
SPIDERLINGS

An adult female wolf spider spins silk. Then she wraps it around her eggs. When she is done, her eggs are safe in an egg sac. It is the size of a pea.

egg sac

She carries the egg sac with her! Why? She protects it from **predators**. She will not leave it unguarded.

CHAPTER 2

More than 100 **spiderlings** hatch from the egg sac. They stay with mom. They ride on her back for two weeks or longer! They grow big enough to hunt for themselves. Then they live on their own.

DID YOU KNOW?

As wolf spiders grow, they **shed** their hard **exoskeletons** many times. They form new ones that fit their larger bodies. This is called molting.

CHAPTER 2

CHAPTER 3
CHASING PREY

A wolf spider's eight eyes watch. Two are on the top of its head! The spider sees really well.

It uses its good eyesight to hunt at night. It catches **insects** and other spiders. Some wolf spiders even eat toads.

CHAPTER 3

Wolf spiders get their name from the way they hunt. They use their long legs to chase prey. They **pounce** to catch it, just like wolves do! Then they suck up the prey's insides.

TAKE A LOOK!

How does a wolf spider eat? Take a look!

❶ A wolf spider catches prey.

❷ The spider sinks its fangs into the prey. Venom goes into the prey.

❸ The prey's insides turn to liquid. The wolf spider sucks it out!

MOUTH

Wolf spiders are almost everywhere. They eat many insects. They keep our **environment** healthy and balanced. Thanks, wolf spiders!

CHAPTER 3

ACTIVITIES & TOOLS

TRY THIS!

SEE AND COMPARE

The Carolina wolf spider's leg span is about three inches (7.6 cm). Measure how objects compare in size with this fun activity!

What You Need:
- ruler
- pencil and paper
- household objects of different sizes

1. Measure and mark three inches (7.6 cm) on a piece of paper. Label it, "Carolina wolf spider leg span."

2. Find some household objects. Make sure they are different sizes! They can include a paper clip, pen, and hairbrush.

3. Measure the objects on your sheet of paper. How big are they? How do they compare to the Carolina wolf spider's leg span? What does this tell you about the spider?

GLOSSARY

arachnid: A creature with a body divided into two parts, such as a spider or a scorpion.

burrows: Tunnels or holes in the ground used as animal homes.

environment: The natural surroundings of living things, such as the air, land, or ocean.

exoskeletons: Hard protective or supporting structures on the outside of arachnids' bodies.

grasslands: Large, open areas of grass.

insects: Small animals with three pairs of legs, one or two pairs of wings, and three main body parts.

leg span: The distance between the tips of a spider's legs.

pounce: To jump forward and grab something suddenly.

predators: Animals that hunt other animals for food.

prey: Animals hunted by other animals for food.

shed: To lose or get rid of something.

species: One of the groups into which similar animals and plants are divided.

spiderlings: Baby spiders.

sprints: Runs fast for a short distance.

venom: Poison.

ACTIVITIES & TOOLS

INDEX

bite 7
burrows 10
Carolina wolf spider 7
chelicerae 8, 9
coloring 5
egg sac 12, 13, 15
exoskeletons 15
eye 9, 16, 17
fangs 7, 8, 9, 19
hunt 15, 17, 18

insects 17, 20
legs 4, 8, 9, 18
molting 15
pounce 18
predators 13
prey 8, 18, 19
silk 12
species 5
spiderlings 15
venom 7, 19

TO LEARN MORE

Finding more information is as easy as 1, 2, 3.

① **Go to www.factsurfer.com**
② **Enter "wolfspiders" into the search box.**
③ **Choose your book to see a list of websites.**

ACTIVITIES & TOOLS